Explore, Discover, Connect!

AN EARLY-CHILDHOOD SERIES FOR CREATIVE THEME DAYS

Connecting with My Community

by Sandra Siegel Plattner

Fearon Teacher Aids

Simon & Schuster Supplementary Education Group

The *Explore, Discover, Connect!* series is dedicated to my family—Jim, Tim, Ken, and Chelsea. Their love and support have made this insurmountable goal become a reality. Thanks, too, to Lorna Abrahams for her help with the initial manuscript.

Editorial Director: Virginia L. Murphy

Series Editors: Marilyn Trow, Sue Mogard, Lisa Schwimmer

Copyeditor: Kristin Eclov

Design: Terry McGrath

Cover and Inside Illustration: Janet Skiles

Cover Design: Lucyna Green

Production: Cletus Coble

ISBN-0-8224-3912-3

Printed in the United States of America

1. 9 8 7 6 5 4 3 2

Contents

A Word About the Series

Explore, Discover, Connect! is an early-childhood series for creative theme days that opens new worlds of information to young children. Hands-on activities invite children to explore their natural curiosities and discover a connection between learned concepts and the world around them. The process of discovering these connections provides opportunities for children to create their own learning, which is so important to building understanding. The activities further integrate all subject areas by helping children develop the following skills:

language arts	listening, speaking, writing, reading
math	counting, sorting, classifying, identifying patterns
science	observing, researching, recording data
social science	interacting with others, discovering similarities and differences among different people
art	exploring color and design
music	interpreting rhythms, hearing different tones
physical education	moving in beneficial ways, toning both large and small muscles

Six main themes integral to early-childhood curriculum form the basis for the *Explore, Discover, Connect!* series. Each theme is explored through a separate book. Pick and choose individual themes that enhance your present curriculum, or gain a comprehensive early-childhood curriculum using all of the books in the series!

Connecting with Myself offers opportunities for children to discover new aspects about themselves through a variety of self-awareness activities.

Connecting with My Community encourages children to make a connection with their immediate community.

Connecting with Holidays gives children a chance to experience the significance of holidays and the fun of celebrating special days together.

Connecting with Nature invites children into the world of nature through the exciting exploration of some of its wonders.

Connecting with the Seasons helps the children discover the many changes in the environment through a yearly cycle.

Connecting Around the World introduces children to different cultures, people, and places all over the world.

Explore, Discover, Connect! was developed with you, the instructor, in mind. A large variety of age-appropriate experiences provides you with the options necessary to meet the diverse needs of the children in your care.

I invite you to enjoy the *Explore, Discover, Connect!* series with your children. Explore the thematic units already prepared and tested, discover the fun and excitement of encouraging children to create their own learning, and connect the newfound spontaneity of lesson planning with the success of teaching concepts through the development of understanding.

Sandra Siegel Plattner

Using the Activities

Children explore the theme of this book through five different topics. The activities for each topic are organized in three easily defined sections to fit the social, emotional, physical, and intellectual needs of early-childhood learners. The activities in each section reinforce the theme and provide developmentally appropriate experiences for the early-childhood learner.

OPENING ACTIVITIES involve the children immediately into the spirit of the theme using fingerplays, songs, motor movement activities, stories, and games.

CENTER ACTIVITIES provide a block of time when children are encouraged to interact with materials in different interest areas. The children also have opportunities to interact socially. The following are suggested interest areas or centers to include daily:

- a dramatic-play center equipped with dress-up clothing and items to encourage role-playing and pretending

- a library corner complete with books, a tape recorder, headsets, and cassette tapes

- a block center with a variety of sizes of blocks

- an art center with an easel, paints, a large table, and materials for writing, drawing, or coloring

- a manipulatives center where a variety of toys are available, such as blocks, puzzles, beads for stringing, and similar items, that encourage the development and strengthening of fine motor skills

- a science center with items from the environment for children to explore

OUTDOOR ACTIVITIES promote the use of the open space necessary to enhance the development of large motor skills. Unstructured and structured activities are suggested for use during this time.

A Suggested Daily Schedule

Opening Activities	20 minutes
Center Activities	45 minutes
Snack	20 minutes
Outdoor Activities	45 minutes
Closing Storytime	20 minutes

The flexibility built into *Connecting with My Community* adds excitement and fun to the learning process. Each topic section is introduced with a supporting statement showing how the activities in that section connect to the overall theme. In addition, a concept-discovery statement for each activity clearly defines the connection children are encouraged to discover within the topics. This format enables you to confidently select those topics and activities that best meet the specific needs and interests of your particular group of children.

Connecting with My Community may be explored fully by systematically presenting each topic, or the topics may be rearranged and spread out over an entire year. Topics may coincide with a special event or holiday season. Be creative and enjoy connecting with the special interests and diverse needs of the children in your care. You are invited to include activities of your own as well.

Children continually learn more about themselves through experiences shared with those nearest them—their community. By exploring a variety of community tasks, the children will begin to develop an interest in their community as well. The activities in *Connecting with My Community* invite the children to explore and experience some of the varied aspects of community life. In an effort to remain child-centered and developmentally appropriate, the objectives of this program are continually reconnecting the activities to the children and their needs. Make learning meaningful and fun!

Let's Play Dentist

The children will discover more about themselves as they learn about good dental care, dental health, and the work of the dentist in the community.

"I know I have baby teeth now, but I will have permanent teeth when I am older."

"I know a dentist takes care of my teeth."

"I know my tongue, jaws, and teeth help me chew my food."

"I know brushing my teeth helps to keep them healthy."

"I know how to brush my teeth after eating."

"I can remember to brush my teeth."

"I know that some foods help keep my teeth clean."

"I know a dentist is a special community helper."

"I know what a dentist does."

"I can eat healthy snacks."

"I know what foods keep my teeth healthy."

"I like my dentist."

"I can smile a really big smile when my teeth are clean!"

OPENING ACTIVITIES

Fingerplay

Brushing My Teeth

Up and down and 'round and 'round (move your finger up and
    down and around in a brushing motion),
I brush my teeth to keep them sound.
To keep them safe and clean and white (point to your teeth),
I brush them morning, noon, and night.

Song

"Get My Toothpaste, Get My Brush"
(Sung to the tune of "Twinkle, Twinkle, Little Star")

Get my toothpaste, get my brush.
I won't hurry, I won't rush.
Working hard to keep teeth clean,
Front and back and in-between.
When I brush for quite a while,
I will have a happy smile!

Hide the Tooth from the Tooth Fairy

"I know I have baby teeth now, but I will have permanent teeth when I am older."

Survey the class to see if any of the children have lost one or more baby teeth. Explain that it is a natural process to lose one's baby teeth. We have two sets of teeth! The first set of teeth are called *baby teeth*. Explain to the children that once we lose our baby teeth, permanent teeth grow in to replace the baby teeth we have lost. Reassure the children who have not lost any baby teeth yet that there is no correct time for children to lose their baby teeth. Children lose their baby teeth at different ages—generally around five, six, or seven.

Invite those children who have lost baby teeth to share their experiences. Ask the children what they did with the teeth that came out. Encourage the children who have not lost any teeth yet to try to imagine what it will be like when they lose their first tooth.

Invite the children to discuss what stories they have heard about the tooth fairy. Make a tooth pattern from white construction paper. Show the tooth to the children. Then invite the children to hide the construction-paper tooth from the tooth fairy. Select one child to role-play the tooth fairy. Have the tooth fairy leave the classroom with an adult helper or older student. While they are gone, invite the other children to sit with you in a circle on the floor. Select one child to sit on the tooth. When the tooth fairy and helper return, encourage the children to give clues that will help the tooth fairy correctly identify the child sitting on the tooth—the color of the child's hair and clothes, the position of the child in the circle, the sex of the child, how the child is sitting, and so on. When the child sitting on the tooth is discovered, that child is invited to become the next tooth fairy.

CENTER ACTIVITIES

Toothy Puppets

"I know a dentist takes care of my teeth."

Materials
   paper plates
   crayons or felt-tip pens
   pieces of white scrap paper
   glue
   hand mirrors

Explain to the children that it is important for everyone to visit the dentist regularly. A dentist will clean and check every tooth to make sure there are no cavities. Explain that a cavity is a sick part of a tooth and that regular visits to the dentist can help prevent cavities (dentists recommend that children have two annual visits). Have the children raise their hands if they have ever visited the dentist. Invite the children to share their experiences. Ask the children if the dentist showed them how to brush their teeth. Also ask if the dentist told the children why it's so important to take care of their teeth. Explain to the children that the dentist helps to keep their teeth happy and healthy. Encourage each child to turn to his or her neighbor and show them a big smile.

Invite the children to make toothy puppets. Give each child a paper plate. Place white scrap pieces of paper and glue within easy reach of the children. Show the children how to fold the paper plates in half so the plates open and shut like mouths. Have the children draw faces on the top half of their plates. Then help the children glue white pieces of scrap paper along the inside rim of the paper-plate mouths to represent teeth.

Encourage the children to count their own teeth with the help of hand mirrors or a friend and then glue the same number of teeth on their paper-plate puppets. Caution the children not to put their fingers in each other's mouths. Just in case, have the children wash their hands before this activity. Interested children may use felt-tip pens or crayons to draw tongues or other details on their puppets, too.

Invite the children to work their toothy puppets by holding them in one hand and making them talk. Help the children compare the number of teeth in each puppet's mouth.

Toothy Smile

"I know my tongue, jaws, and teeth help me chew my food."

Materials
    red playdough or modeling clay (a recipe is provided)
    white navy beans
    model or diagram of the mouth (borrow from a dentist, if possible)

Show the children a model of the mouth, complete with teeth, tongue, and jaw. Point out the position of the teeth, tongue, and jaw inside the mouth. Using the model, or your own mouth, demonstrate how the alignment of the jaws and teeth help us chew. Invite the children to open and close their mouths to feel the alignment of their teeth and jaws as well. Have the children wash their hands before this activity.

Use red playdough to make models of a mouth. Suggest that the children insert white navy beans in the dough for teeth. Place the dentist's model of a mouth nearby for reference as the children work. This can be an independent activity for older children—younger children will need teacher assistance. When the dough has hardened, display the models in the classroom for several days. Then invite the children to take the models home to share with their families.

Playdough Recipe

2 cups flour
1 cup salt
1 tsp cream of tartar
2 cups cold water
4 Tbsp oil
2 Tbsp food coloring

Mix the flour, salt, and cream of tartar in a bowl. Gradually stir in the water. Put the mixture in an electric skillet. Add oil and red food coloring. Cook the mixture over medium heat, stirring constantly until a ball forms. Be sure to cook out of the reach of children. Caution the children to stand back, since the skillet is hot. Remove the hot playdough from the skillet and let it cool. Then divide the playdough into smaller balls. Invite the children to knead the playdough once it has cooled properly.

Brush Away the Yellow

"I know brushing my teeth helps to keep them healthy."

Materials
- white paint smocks
- old toothbrushes
- yellow construction-paper tooth patterns
- white tempera paint

Discuss how important it is for the children to brush and floss their teeth correctly. Explain that proper brushing and flossing is necessary to remove the tiny pieces of food and any germs on teeth. Point out that teeth can become yellowed when they are not brushed regularly and correctly. Keeping teeth clean helps reduce the chance of getting cavities. In addition to daily brushing, dentists also advise having check-ups and teeth cleaned twice a year. Explain that dentists have special tools to clean the teeth.

Demonstrate the correct way to brush and floss the teeth. Or, if possible, have a dental assistant or dental hygienist come visit the classroom and demonstrate good dental care. Then invite the children to practice brushing teeth on large yellow construction-paper tooth patterns. Place several yellow construction-paper tooth patterns on a paint easel. Invite the children to take turns role-playing dentists. Give them white paint smocks to wear while they "clean" the yellow teeth using old toothbrushes and white paint. Encourage the children to brush the teeth properly. Caution the children not to put the old toothbrushes in their mouths. Point out the importance of never using another person's toothbrush because of the germs in our mouths. Display the "cleaned" teeth in a row on a bulletin board in the classroom to make a gleaming, healthy smile.

Preventing Cavities

"I know how to brush my teeth after eating."

Materials
- several cooked and cleaned chicken bones
- glass
- soda pop

Explain that one way children may prevent cavities is to brush their teeth after eating—especially after drinking or eating sweet foods. Sweet drinks and foods are especially high in sugar. Point out that a bowl of sugar-coated breakfast cereal, for example, contains more sugar than a candy bar! Sugar, if left on the teeth, can cause cavities. Send a letter home explaining the purpose of this activity so parents can be prepared for questions or reactions regarding sugary foods. Be aware that some children may even become afraid of "sugary" foods.

To demonstrate the effect of sugar on teeth, put several cooked and cleaned chicken bones into a glass of soda pop. Explain that the soda pop contains sugar. Leave the bones in the soda for one week. At the end of the week, invite the children to observe the results. Point out to the children that although sugar does not directly come in contact with their bones and will not hurt their bones, sugar does come in contact with their teeth. It is important to remove sugar from teeth by brushing regularly!

Toothbrushing Records

"I can remember to brush my teeth."

Ask the children how many times a day they brush their teeth. Point out that, ideally, they should brush their teeth after every meal. Explain that it is especially important for them to brush their teeth before going to bed at night. Any bits of food left on their teeth when they go to bed will stay there all night, which is not healthy for their teeth.

Make charts for the children to take home and use to record the number of times each day they brush their teeth for one week. Send a letter of explanation home to parents or guardians encouraging them to help their children keep track of toothbrushing records for one week. Request that parents return the completed charts to school. To provide for children who do not return their toothbrushing records, have several sample charts available so these children can fill them out at school. At the end of the week, help each child add the daily and weekly totals. Point out to the children that brushing their teeth is one of the best things they can do to help dentists keep their teeth healthy and strong.

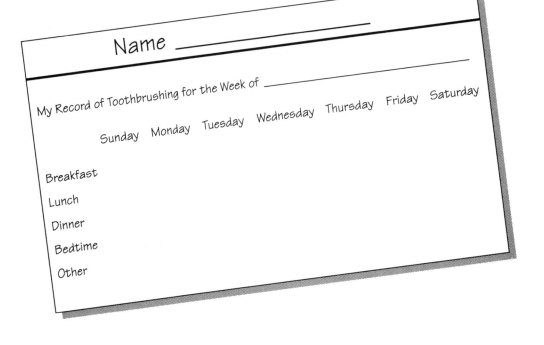

Name _____

My Record of Toothbrushing for the Week of _____

	Sunday	Monday	Tuesday	Wednesday	Thursday	Friday	Saturday
Breakfast							
Lunch							
Dinner							
Bedtime							
Other							

Natural Toothbrushes

"I know that some foods help keep my teeth clean."

Materials
- carrots
- celery
- apples
- carrot peelers
- bowl
- aprons
- knife (adult use only)

Explain that even though we know it is important to brush our teeth after every meal and snack, it is not always possible to do so. Point out that carrots, celery, and apples, as well as other fruits and vegetables low in sugar, help to naturally clean our teeth. Eating these foods at the end of a meal can help keep our teeth clean when it isn't possible to use a toothbrush. Rinsing our mouths with water following a meal also helps to remove trapped food and sugar from our teeth.

Invite the children to help prepare healthy snacks. Remind the children to first wash their hands. Also have the children wash the carrots, apples, and celery for the snack. Show the children how to carefully use the peelers to clean the carrots. As you model the correct method of peeling carrots, explain to the children what you are doing. Have an adult volunteer monitor the children as they use the peelers. Caution the children to always move the peelers away from their bodies while peeling rather than towards them. Invite the children to take turns peeling carrots. Have an adult volunteer cut the carrots, celery, and apples into bite-size pieces. Invite the children to enjoy eating these healthy snacks!

Dentist's Visit

"I know a dentist is a special community helper."

Materials
   drawing paper
   felt-tip pens or crayons

Invite a dentist (or dental hygienist) to come visit the the classroom or preschool and demonstrate good dental care, as well as the different work he or she performs. Write down the different jobs performed by the dentist or dental hygienist on chart paper to refer to after the visit. Encourage the dentist to also suggest foods that help keep teeth healthy. Suggest that the dentist bring along any models or small equipment he or she uses in dental work to share with the children as well. Ask the dentist to stress that dental care is everyone's responsibility.

Following the visit, review with the children some of the different work that a dentist performs—reading from the list on the chart paper. Then invite the children to draw pictures of dentists doing different tasks. Have the children dictate any comments they would like added to the bottom of their pictures. Compile the pictures into a booklet entitled "The Dentist: A Special Community Helper." Place the booklet in the library center for children to enjoy during independent time.

Dental Office

"I know what a dentist does."

If possible, arrange for the children to view a filmstrip, video, or film about a visit to the dentist. Discuss the different tasks dentists do during a typical day. Besides cleaning and repairing teeth, point out that the dentist also makes caps for teeth and false teeth, too.

Set up a dental office in the dramatic-play area in your classroom using the props and ideas suggested here. Invite the children to use the props to role-play visits to a dentist. Caution the children to only pretend to work in each other's mouths. Explain to children the importance of not putting their hands in their own mouths or in another person's mouth. Germs can be easily spread when hands are not clean. Point out that a real dentist uses gloves and sterile equipment when working in the mouth of a patient. Encourage the children to take turns role-playing the dentist, patients, and lab assistants.

Suggested Roles, Props, and Ideas for a Dental Dramatic-Play Area

Dentist
  chair with a T.V. tray next to it
  paper towels and clothespins
  dental instruments
  large teeth patterns
  toothbrush
  white coat
  rubber gloves

Lab Assistant
  table
  model of a mouth
  playdough
  lab coat

Healthy Snacks

"I can eat healthy snacks."

Materials

nuts, dried fruit, cubes of cheese, vegetable sticks, popcorn,
  and other similar foods that have no added sugar
large sheet of tagboard
construction paper
magazine pictures of food
glue
scissors

Invite the children to name the snacks they most enjoy eating. Make a list of the snacks the children name on a large sheet of tagboard. Ask the children to help you decide which snacks on the list contain a lot of sugar and which ones do not. Circle all the healthier snacks and discuss their benefits to maintaining healthy teeth.

Offer the sugarless snacks to the children, such as dried fruit, vegetable sticks, cheese, and so on. Give each child a sheet of construction paper. Encourage the children to fold the paper in half to make two sections. Invite the children to cut out two magazine pictures of sugary snacks, such as cake or cookies, and two pictures of healthy snacks, such as raisins or cheese. Glue the healthy-snack pictures on one half of the paper and the sugary snack pictures on the other half. Display the pictures around the room. Encourage the children to eat healthy snacks at home. Suggest that they keep track of the healthy snacks enjoyed by their families. Keep in mind that many processed foods also contain sugar.

Happy or Sad Teeth?

"I know what foods keep my teeth healthy."

Materials

      pictures of foods that contain added sugar

      pictures of foods that contain little or no added sugar

      a large cutout of a tooth with a sad face drawn on it

      a large cutout of a tooth with a happy face drawn on it

Show the children a cutout of a tooth with a sad face drawn on it. Encourage the children to suggest why the tooth is sad. Then show the children the happy tooth cutout. Encourage the children to suggest possible reasons why this tooth is happy. Accept all suggestions. When you do not understand a child's answer, invite further explanation. Pin the happy and sad teeth on a bulletin board.

Explain that it is okay for children to eat some sweet foods, as long as they brush their teeth after eating. Show the children the food pictures. Discuss whether the food in each picture contains a lot of sugar, a little sugar, or no sugar. Point out that those foods with little or no sugar added generally make teeth the happiest. Give each child a food picture. Encourage each child to name the food in the picture and decide whether it will make teeth happy or sad. Invite the children to put their pictures by the appropriate tooth on the bulletin board. Following this activity, place the pictures and teeth in a learning center for independent time.

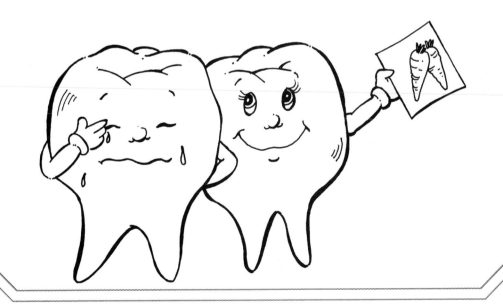

OUTDOOR ACTIVITIES

A Visit to the Dentist

"I like my dentist."

Arrange for the children to visit a local dental office. Be sure to obtain signed field-trip permission slips from the children's parents. Before the visit, discuss the different instruments and people the children may see there. Rehearse with the children some questions they may ask during the visit. During the tour of the office, invite the children to ask any questions they may have. If permissible, encourage the children to explore the examination areas and sit in a patient's chair. Think of other ways that you can help the children feel comfortable as well.

After the visit, discuss any additional questions the children may have. Invite the children to draw pictures for their new friend and community helper—the dentist. Send the pictures to the dentist as a special thank-you.

Flash a Healthy Smile Walk

"I can smile a really big smile when my teeth are clean!"

Materials
 safety pins
 4" paper circles
 crayons
 felt-tip pens
 camera and film

Discuss how good it feels to smile when we know our teeth are healthy and clean. On a designated day, plan to take the children on a walk around the neighborhood. Before going on the walk, obtain signed field-trip permission slips from the children's parents. Make "We Love Dentists" badges for the children to wear on the walk. Have an adult volunteer write the slogan on each badge. Invite the children to decorate their badges as well. Then have adult volunteers pin the badges on the children's clothing with safety pins. Encourage the children to show really big smiles at one another and at everyone they meet along the way! Take a photograph of the children with their badges and include a copy with thank-you pictures you'd like to send to the dentist (see *A Visit to the Dentist* on page 22). Place another copy of the photograph on the classroom bulletin board.

Little Chef

Children become little chefs, learning the importance of preparing nutritious foods in special ways, as they discover different food service groups in the community.

"I know a chef knows how to pick the best fruits."
"I know there are lots of ways to eat potatoes."
"I know that fruits are good for me."
"I know corn grows from little seeds."
"I know that a chef's salad is big enough for a meal!"
"I know I am supposed to wash my hands and wear an apron when I cook."
"I know chefs wear special hats when they cook."
"I can make cinnamon toast just like a chef."
"I can make peanut butter."
"I can make fresh orange juice."
"I know many vegetables help make vegetable soup."
"I know a grocery store is a busy place."
"I know what food looks like and tastes like."
"I know how to set the table."
"I know how vegetables look and feel."
"I know some fresh fruits and vegetables are crunchy and some are soft."

"I can help plant and grow a vegetable garden."
"I know growing a garden is a big job."
"I know the names of lots of foods."
"I can help feed the animals in my community."
"I know apples grow in an orchard."
"I know grocery store workers take care of the food in the store."
"I know a baker is a special kind of chef."
"I know what the different workers do in a restaurant."

OPENING ACTIVITIES

Fingerplay

Pantomime the actions in the following fingerplay.

I am making cookie dough.
'Round and 'round the beaters go.
Add some ingredients from a cup.
Stir and stir the batter up.
Roll it, cut cookies nice and neat.
Put them on a cookie sheet.
Bake them, count them, "One, two, three!"
Serve them to a friend for tea.

Fresh Fruit

"I know a chef knows how to pick the best fruits."

Materials
   a selection of seasonal fruits (at least two of each kind of fruit—
      include some over-ripe and under-ripe fruits as well)
   chart paper
   felt-tip pen
   knife (adult use only)
   large bowl
   serving spoon
   plastic spoons
   paper plates

Ask the children to name several different kinds of fruit. Record all of the ideas on chart paper. Explain that fruits are an important part of our diet. Survey the class to find out the children's favorite fruits. You could develop a simple bar graph to show the results of the survey. Point out that when a chef prepares fruit dishes, only the best fruit is used. Then, on the menu, the fruits and other foods are deliciously described to encourage people to order these foods.

Before beginning this activity, invite all children to thoroughly wash their hands. Point out that hand washing reduces the spread of germs and that all chefs wash their hands repeatedly before and as they handle food. Show the children a selection of fresh fruit. Include some under-ripe and over-ripe fruit in the selection as well. Invite children to talk about the similarities and differences in the over-ripe and under-ripe fruits. Talk about which are the best to use for food preparation and why.

Invite the children to role-play chefs and select the best fruit to use at their restaurant. Encourage the children to smell, feel, and examine each kind of fruit before making their selections. Once their selections have been made, help the children describe the fruit as it might appear on a menu. For example, an apple might be described as sweet, juicy, ripe, and so on. Invite the children to carefully wash each piece of ripe fruit. Have an adult volunteer cut the fruit into bite-size pieces and place in a large bowl. Give each child a paper plate and a plastic spoon. Invite the children to take a serving spoonful of the delicious fruit salad. Be sure a spoon is never returned to the bowl if it ends up in a child's mouth.

Hot Potato

"I know there are lots of ways to eat potatoes."

Materials
>   record and record player
>   different varieties of potatoes

Show the children several different kinds of potatoes, such as new potatoes, sweet potatoes, white potatoes, and red potatoes. Point out that potatoes are usually served hot. Ask the children to name as many different ways of preparing potatoes as possible—mashed, baked, fried, scalloped, and so on. Ask the children to name their favorite way to eat potatoes.

Invite the children to sit with you in a circle on the floor to play the game "Hot Potato." Ask one child to select an object to be the potato for the game. Have the children pretend that the selected potato just came out of the chef's oven and is very hot. Explain that when you begin to play some music, the children are to pass the "hot" potato quickly around the circle. When the music stops, the child left holding the potato must go into the middle of the circle to "cool" his or her hands. The game then begins again. The child sitting in the middle of the circle may rejoin the rest of the children when he or she is replaced by the next child caught holding the potato that is "hot!"

Fruit Basket Upset

"I know that fruits are good for me."

Materials
> pictures of different kinds of fruits (two of each fruit)
> safety pins
> chart of the four basic food groups

Show the children a chart of the four basic food groups. Discuss how the foods from each group work together to keep our bodies healthy. Explain that when meals are planned for restaurants or schools, the chef or cook tries to serve a food from each of the four food groups. Chefs, for example, try to use a variety of fresh fruits to add color and taste to the meals they serve. Point out that fruits are an important part of each meal.

Show the children pictures of the different fruits. Help the children identify each one. Then invite each child to choose a favorite fruit picture, making sure that two pictures of each kind of fruit are chosen. Help the children pin the fruit pictures on their clothing. Call out the names of the different fruits one at a time. Invite the children to stand as you say the pictured fruits they wear. When all the children are standing, ask them to get chairs and make a circle in an open area of the classroom.

Explain that you need the children's help to make an imaginary fruit salad. You will role-play the chef and the children will role-play the fruit. Point out that a chef makes fruit salad by mixing many different kinds of fruit together. Explain that when you say the names of the various fruits, the children wearing pictures of those fruits must get up and move to other chairs. Practice with each type of fruit and then say "Fruit basket upset!" At this signal, invite all of the children to move to other chairs!

Sing and Act Out

"I know corn grows from little seeds."

Ask the children if they know where corn comes from before it is prepared for them to eat. Explain the life cycle of corn—from seed, to seedling, to plant, to "fruit" of the plant, to the harvesting of the corn. If possible, provide pictures depicting each stage. Discuss how the farmer gets the corn to the store and then how it is purchased by a chef. Teach the children the following song, inviting them to pantomime the actions.

"How the Farmers Grow Corn"
(Sung to the tune of "Here We Go 'Round the Mulberry Bush")

First the farmers plow the earth,
Plow the earth, plow the earth.
First the farmers plow the earth,
Then they plant the seeds.

This is the way they plant the seeds,
Plant the seeds, plant the seeds.
This is the way they plant the seeds,
So that they will grow.

The rain and sun will help them grow,
Help them grow, help them grow.
The rain and sun will help them grow,
Right up through the ground.

Now the farmers pick the corn,
Pick the corn, pick the corn.
Now the farmers pick the corn,
And we have food to eat.

Trucks carry the corn to the store,
To the store, to the store.
Trucks carry the corn to the store,
So we can buy it there.

CENTER ACTIVITIES

Chef's Salad

"I know that a chef's salad is big enough for a meal!"

Ask the children to name the ingredients in their favorite salads—lettuce, carrots, celery, and so on. Explain that because salads are usually less filling than many foods, they are frequently served at the beginning of a meal. However, some salads are large enough to eat as meals, such as chef salads, fajitas, taco salads, and so on. Ask the children if they can name other salad meals as well. A chef's salad is a big bowl full of regular salad ingredients, plus eggs, meat, and cheese. A chef's salad is a meal in itself!

Make a pretend chef's salad. Invite the children to sit with you in a circle on the floor. Set a large salad bowl in the center of the circle. Begin by saying, "In the salad is a (tomato)." Invite the child sitting on your right to then "add" another ingredient by saying, "I will add a (carrot)." Continue around the circle, helping the group repeat the ingredients previously named and then inviting the children in turn to add new ingredients. At different times, encourage interested children to try to name all of the items in the salad by themselves. When all the ingredients have been added, invite the children to pretend to eat.

Getting Ready to Cook

"I know I am supposed to wash my hands and wear an apron when I cook."

Materials

    ribbon (cut in lengths that may be tied around a child's waist)
    different colors of construction paper (cut in large rectangles)
    felt-tip pens or crayons
    stapler

Explain that before handling any food, a chef washes his or her hands with soap and water and puts on an apron. Hands may carry germs, and washing one's hands helps keep germs away from food. Point out that an apron protects a chef's clothing. But it also keeps any germs on the chef's clothing away from the food as well. Stress that every chef must wear something to cover his or her clothing and must always have clean hands when handling and preparing food.

Invite the children to make chefs' aprons. Give each child a large rectangle cut from colored construction paper and a length of ribbon (measure to make sure the ribbon is long enough to tie around the child's waist). Have the children decorate the rectangles using felt-tip pens or crayons. Then, help the children lay the ribbon out straight on a long table or the floor. Position the rectangle in the middle of the ribbon. Staple the rectangles to the ribbons. Suggest that children wear their aprons when they pretend to prepare foods in the kitchen dramatic-play area.

Chef's Hat

"I know chefs wear special hats when they cook."

Materials
   paper bags (one per child)
   long strips of construction paper
   shredded newspaper
   stapler
   felt-tip pens

Show the children a picture of a chef wearing a tall, white chef's hat. Or, show the children a real chef's hat if one is available. Ask the children if they know why chefs wear a hat while preparing food. Explain that chefs with long hair also wear a hair net. Point out that hair strands can easily fall into food unless a hat or hair net is worn. Encourage the children to observe the food servers at fast-food restaurants when they eat out with their families to see the different types of hats or hair nets the food servers wear.

Invite the children to make chefs' hats. Give each child a paper bag to first decorate and then stuff half full with shredded newspaper. Measure and cut strips of construction paper to fit around each child's head. Then help the children carefully staple the strips around the sacks, about three inches from the opening of the bags. Invite the children to wear their hats during lunch one day just for fun!

Cinnamon Toast

"I can make cinnamon toast just like a chef."

Materials
   bread
   margarine
   cinnamon sugar in shaker bottles
   butter knives
   cookie sheets
   aprons

Point out that chefs often need to prepare large amounts of food at one time. For example, for breakfast, a chef may need to prepare a hundred or more slices of toast! Help the children come up with a list of different ways to toast one hundred slices of bread at one time.

Invite the children to watch as you experiment with toasting bread in the oven. Remind the children to wash their hands and put on aprons before handling the food. Give each child a slice of bread to butter and sprinkle with cinnamon sugar. Set the oven to "broil." Arrange the prepared slices of bread on cookie sheets. Be sure to keep the children away from the hot oven. Carefully place the cookie sheets on the top rack. Set a timer for a few minutes to show the children how quickly the bread is toasted. Invite the children to enjoy a group snack of warm cinnamon toast!

Peanut Butter

"I can make peanut butter."

Materials
   1 lb unshelled peanuts
   vegetable oil
   bread
   jelly
   blender
   aprons
   butter knives
   large bowl

Explain that many packaged foods found on grocery store shelves may be made from ingredients found in the kitchen cupboard. Show the children a jar of peanut butter. Point out that peanut butter may be made with just two ingredients. Encourage the children to guess what two ingredients are found in peanut butter (peanut butter is made from vegetable oil and peanuts).

Invite the children to make peanut butter. Cover a table with newspaper. Remind the children to wash their hands and put on aprons before handling the peanuts. Invite the children to help shell the peanuts. Have the children place the unshelled peanuts in a large bowl. Stress the importance of removing all of the peanut shells and skins before making peanut butter. Have an adult volunteer pour the bowl of shelled peanuts into the blender. Be sure the blender is kept out of the reach of children.

Gather the children on the floor a safe distance from the blender. Show the children the peanuts in the blender before mixing. Encourage the children to predict what will happen when you turn on the blender. Periodically stop blending and show the children what is happening to the peanuts inside the blender. Add vegetable oil as needed to make the peanut butter a spreadable consistency. Invite the children to make peanut butter and jelly sandwiches. Homemade peanut butter makes a tasty snack!

Orange Juice

"I can make fresh orange juice."

Materials
   - fresh oranges
   - orange juice squeezers
   - aprons
   - newspaper
   - knife (adult use only)
   - pitcher
   - measuring cup
   - 3-oz paper cups

Point out that fresh foods always contain the most nutrients. Nutrients are those vitamins and minerals in foods that bodies need to grow and function properly. Explain that whenever the children eat fresh fruits or vegetables, they are getting the best nutrients for building healthy bodies. Point out that canned or frozen foods are good for them as well, but some of the nutrients have been taken away and often something artificial has been added.

Invite the children to make freshly squeezed orange juice. Orange juice is rich in vitamin C. Explain that fresh orange juice is very nutritious. Show the children an orange juice squeezer. Challenge the children to predict how many oranges will need to be squeezed to make one cup of juice. Write these predictions on chart paper for later reference.

When all the predictions are in, have an adult volunteer cut the oranges in half and invite the children to help squeeze several oranges. Remind the children to wash their hands and put on aprons beforehand. Keep a tally of how many oranges are used to make one cup of juice. Compare the actual number of oranges squeezed to the children's predictions. Make enough juice for each child to have a small sample.

Vegetable Soup

"I know many vegetables help make vegetable soup."

Materials
- beef broth
- bouillon cube
- potatoes, carrots, celery, peas, beans, onions, carrots, and other vegetables children bring from home
- salt, pepper, parsley, oregano, garlic powder
- large pot or crockpot
- wooden spoon
- knife (adult use only)
- vegetable scrapers
- vegetable peelers
- aprons
- serving spoon or ladle
- small bowls and spoons for each child

Send a letter home with the children asking parents to send one vegetable to school with their children to contribute to a class cooking project. Invite each child to share information with the class about the vegetable he or she brings to school. Suggest that the children describe the color and texture of their vegetables and why they chose these particular vegetables as well.

Read *Stone Soup* by Marcia Brown to the class (see the bibliography on page 92). Explain that chefs often use leftover vegetables to make homemade soup. Invite the children to use the vegetables they bring from home to make their own "Stone Soup." For added fun, use a beef bouillon cube to represent the stone as the first ingredient! Remind the children to wash their hands and put on aprons before handling the vegetables.

Ask the children to help you wash and peel the vegetables. Caution the children to always move the vegetable peelers away from their bodies while peeling rather than towards them. Then have an adult volunteer slice the vegetables and place all the vegetables in a large pot. Add beef broth and seasonings. Be sure to cook out of reach of the children. Bring the ingredients to a boil. Then let the soup simmer for at least an hour. Caution children to stay far away from the hot soup pot and the stove. Point out that the longer the soup simmers, the more the flavor of each vegetable is brought out. Cool the soup slightly before serving.

Grocery Store

"I know a grocery store is a busy place."

Set up a grocery store in the dramatic-play area. Invite the children to help arrange the props suggested here. Discuss the special jobs necessary to operate a grocery store and the many roles available for them to play. Encourage the children to have fun shopping at the store, stocking the shelves with food items, pricing the grocery items, acting as the cashier, and bagging the groceries.

Suggested Props for a Grocery Store Dramatic-Play Area

play cash register
play money
empty boxes of cereal, pasta, and so on
empty cans of soups, fruits, vegetables
    (the can edges need to be taped)
plastic fruits, vegetables, and meat
tables to display groceries
small table for cash register
stickers
paper bags
grocery carts (wagons)
pad of paper
pencils
aprons
chair

Food Pinup

"I know what food looks like and tastes like."

Materials

pictures of a variety of familiar foods
tape

Invite the children to sit with you in a circle on the floor. Tape a food picture to each child's back. Caution the children not to reveal to one another what pictures are on their backs. Ask one child to stand and turn around to show the group the picture on his or her back. Help the other children give clues that will help that child guess what food is pictured. When the child correctly identifies the food, he or she may select another child to stand. Continue until all the food pictures have been identified. As a final review of the foods, go around the circle asking each child to recall, without looking, what food is pictured on his or her back.

Setting the Table

"I know how to set the table."

Materials
  cups
  napkins
  silverware
  placemats
  table
  paper plates

Discuss how sometimes a meal seems more enjoyable when the table is set nicely. Help the children make a list of the items normally used to set the table. Explain that each item has a special place on the table. Point out that the fork is placed on the left side of the plate, the knife and spoon are placed on the right side, and so on. Invite various children to help as you demonstrate how to properly set a table. Then invite each child to practice setting his or her own place setting. Show the children how to fold their napkins in special ways as well. Invite the children to use the table-setting items in the kitchen dramatic-play area to make their meals more special.

Categorizing Vegetables

"I know how vegetables look and feel."

Materials
>   tray of ten different vegetables, such as cucumbers, carrots, radishes,
>   broccoli, beans, cauliflower, peas, lettuce, and so on
>   knife (adult use only)

Display ten different vegetables on a tray. Help the children identify the
vegetables as you point to each one. Discuss the texture, size, and smell
of each vegetable. Invite the children to thoroughly wash their hands,
since they will be handling the different vegetables. Compare the
various vegetables as well, noting likenesses and differences. Encourage
the children to examine each vegetable carefully. Challenge the children
to group the vegetables in as many different categories as possible
according to shared characteristics, such as color, shape, or size.

Then ask the children to take turns closing their eyes and picking up
the vegetables. Using descriptive words, such as bumpy, smooth, round,
and large, encourage the children to correctly identify each one. After
discussing the characteristics or attributes of each vegetable, help the
children arrange the vegetables into categories according to size, shape,
color, texture, smell, and so on. When all ideas are exhausted, have the
children wash the vegetables. Then have an adult volunteer cut the
vegetables into bite-size pieces for the children to enjoy as a nutritious
snack!

Fresh Fruits and Vegetables

"I know some fresh fruits and vegetables are crunchy and some are soft."

Materials
> fresh fruits and vegetables
> serrated knives (adult use only)
> empty margarine tubs or other containers
> (one per fruit or vegetable)

Hold up a fruit and invite the children to share all the information they know about it. Cut the fruit in half and show the children the inside. Point out the seeds and other interior parts. Hold up another fruit or vegetable and repeat the same process. Continue until all the fruits and vegetables have been discussed and cut open. Have an adult volunteer finish cutting the fruits and vegetables into bite-size pieces. Remind the children to wash their hands and put on aprons before handling the fruits and vegetables. Invite the children to help put each fruit and vegetable into a separate container.

Explain that some fresh fruits and vegetables are crunchy when they are fresh and others are soft. For example, a carrot should be crunchy, but a pear should be soft. Encourage the children to predict whether each fruit or vegetable will be crunchy or soft. Make a two-column chart to place beside the food containers. Label one column "Crunchy" and the other column "Soft." As the children sample the fruits and vegetables in the containers, invite them to put tally marks under the headings. Display the finished chart in the classroom. Discuss the results.

OUTDOOR ACTIVITIES

Vegetable Garden

"I can help plant and grow a vegetable garden."

Materials
> packaged vegetable seeds
> watering can
> child-size shovels or digging utensils

Arrange for permission for your class to plant a garden on the preschool or school grounds or on a nearby lot. Send a letter home to the parents explaining the vegetable-garden project. If the garden plot is off school grounds, be sure to obtain signed field-trip permission slips from the children's parents. Point out to the children that every fruit and vegetable bought at the grocery store or eaten in a restaurant is grown in a garden. Help the children make a list of the vegetables they would like to grow. Discuss the length of the growing season needed for each vegetable. You can get this information from your local nursery. Help the children narrow their list to those vegetables that will produce fruit during the time allowed for the project.

Take the children outside to the designated garden plot. Give each child a shovel or other digging utensil. Explain that the soil must be loosened before the seeds may be planted. Invite the children to help dig up the ground to prepare it for the seeds. Show the children how to make rows in the loosened ground and plant the seeds according to the package directions.

Help the children keep a growth chart for each type of vegetable planted. Schedule different children to water and weed the garden daily. Celebrate the appearance of the first green shoot, the first green leaf, and finally the first "fruit" of each plant. Enjoy a fresh snack together as the vegetables are ripe and ready to be harvested.

Peter Rabbit

"I know growing a garden is a big job."

Invite the children to sit with you on the ground in a grassy area outdoors. Encourage the children to discuss the care a garden requires. Ask the children if they know why fences are often built around gardens. Point out that plant-eating animals would find a garden a wonderful place to eat! Ask the children to name some animals that enjoy eating plants. Read *The Complete Adventures of Peter Rabbit* by Beatrix Potter aloud to the children (see the bibliography on page 92). After reading the book, encourage the children to recall their favorite parts. Invite the children to play a game acting out the part of the story when Peter sneaks around Mr. McGregor's vegetable garden.

Invite the children to stand, hold hands, and form a large circle. Designate the inside of the circle as the vegetable garden. Assign one child to role-play Peter Rabbit and another child to role-play Mr. McGregor. Direct Peter to stand inside the circle, pretending to eat the vegetables in Mr. McGregor's garden. Have Mr. McGregor stand outside the circle. Explain that the rest of the children are to help Peter escape from the garden before Mr. McGregor catches him. At the same time, they must prevent Mr. McGregor from catching Peter. The children may help Peter escape and prevent Mr. McGregor from catching Peter by lifting and lowering their arms. When Mr. McGregor catches Peter, choose two new children to role-play the parts.

Food Hop

"I know the names of lots of foods."

Materials
  old window shade
  laminated pictures of different foods
  glue
  masking tape

Draw a hopscotch grid on an old window shade. Tape or glue pictures of different foods in the sections of the grid. Spread the hopscotch game on a smooth surface on the playground. Invite a few children to stand on the edges of the hopscotch shade. Review the names of each food pictured on the grid. Ask the children which pictured food is their favorite. Point out that scientists have put foods into four basic food groups—vegetables and fruits, milk, breads and cereals, and meats and beans. Help the children determine the food group each pictured food belongs in. Explain that it is important to eat foods from each of these four food groups at every meal.

Invite the children to play hopscotch. Select one child to stand at the beginning of the hopscotch grid. Give directions to the child, such as "Hop to the (cheese). Then hop back." While that child hops, encourage the other children to chant, "(Sue) is hopping, hopping, hopping to the (cheese)." Invite the children to cheer when the child reaches the named food. Encourage the children to take turns playing the game. Continue as long as the children are interested. Then make the hopscotch grid available for the children to use both inside and outside the classroom during independent time. Children may use the hopscotch grid independently by simply naming the foods as they hop over them.

Follow the Popcorn Trail

"I can help feed the animals in my community."

Materials

    popcorn kernels
    sunflower seeds (or roasted pumpkin seeds, if in season)

Show the children some popcorn kernels. Explain that plants grow from seeds. Ask the children what plant grows from these seeds. Accept all suggestions, then provide the correct answer. If possible, have a picture of a sunflower for children who have never seen one. Point out that seeds also provide a source of food for some animals. Help the children name different animals that eat seeds. Ask the children if they have ever eaten seeds themselves. Give each child a few sunflower seeds or roasted pumpkin seeds to sample (see the recipe provided on page 48).

Take the children outside to an area that has lots of hiding places. If hiding places do not occur naturally, create them with large boxes or other obstacles. Divide the class into two groups for some hide-and-seek fun. Give the children in one group some popcorn kernels. Instruct the children in the other group to cover their eyes. No fair peeking! Help the group with the seeds leave a trail of popcorn kernels from their starting place to an agreed-upon hiding place. After the trail is made and the children have crouched down to hide, invite the children in the other group to uncover their eyes and follow the popcorn trail. When they get to the hiding place, encourage the discovered children to jump up and yell, "Surprise!" Reverse roles and enjoy the activity all over again.

When the children tire of the game, point out how the birds and other animals will eat the seeds left on the playground so there is no mess to clean up! Then encourage the children to check each day to see if the seeds have been eaten.

Pumpkin-Seed Treats

pumpkin seeds	Invite the children to prepare a pumpkin-seed treat. Preheat an oven to 450°. Remind the children to put
salt	on aprons and wash their hands before handling the
bowl	seeds. Help the children wash the pumpkin seeds
paper towels	thoroughly in a large bowl, then spread the seeds out
cookie sheets	on paper towels to dry. Then have the children place
aprons	the dried pumpkin seeds evenly on a cookie sheet and

lightly sprinkle the seeds with salt. Caution the children to stay away from the hot oven. Put the cookie sheet in a preheated oven and bake the seeds for 10 to 15 minutes, or until the seeds are slightly brown. Once the seeds have cooled sufficiently, invite the children to enjoy the crunchy, nutty-tasting treat!

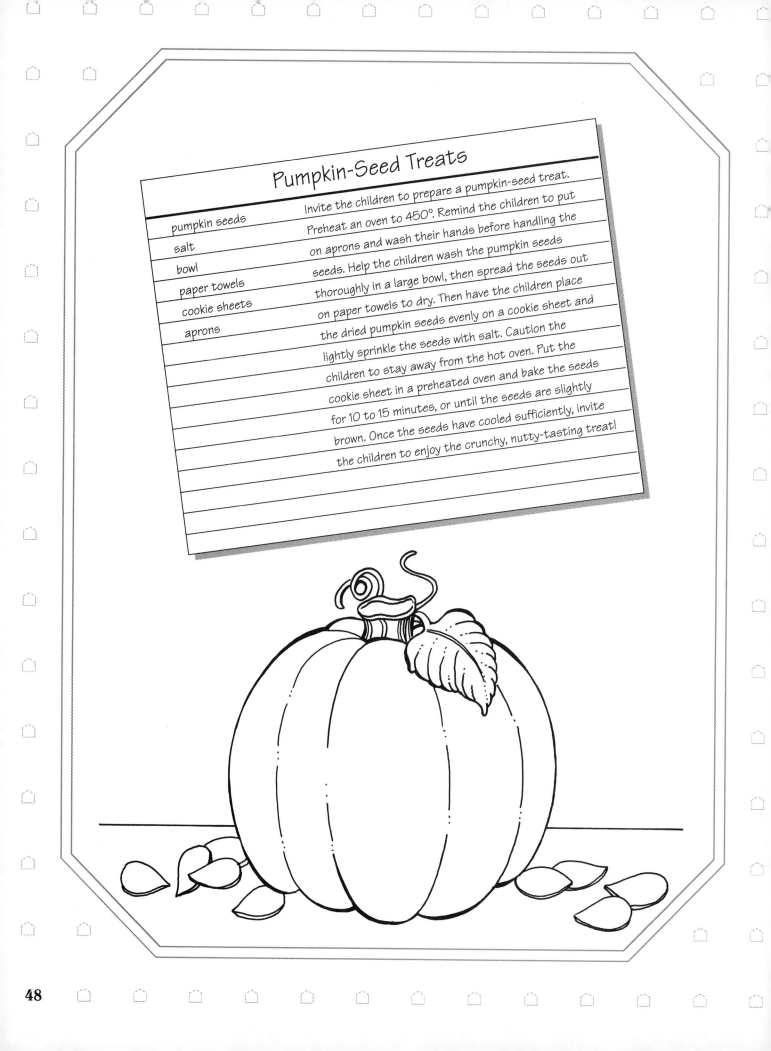

Visit An Apple Orchard

"I know apples grow in an orchard."

Show the children a selection of different kinds of apples. Explain that apples are grown in orchards. An orchard contains hundreds of trees. People are hired to carefully pick the apples. The apples must then be sorted according to their use. Some apples are better for making applesauce. Others are used to make apple juice, apple cider, or canned apples. Many apples are bagged just the way they are for eating.

If an apple orchard is nearby, arrange for the children to visit. Be sure to obtain signed field-trip permission slips from the children's parents. Suggest that your guide show the children the orchard, explain the different varieties of apples, and point out how orchard workers take care of the trees. If possible, invite each child to pick an apple to be enjoyed later at snack time.

Visit a Grocery Store

"I know grocery store workers take care of the food in the store."

Arrange for the class to visit a nearby grocery store. Be sure to obtain signed field-trip permission slips from the children's parents. Beforehand, encourage the children to share how they help their families shop for food at the grocery store. Point out that there are many different jobs at a grocery store. Help the children make a list of the special jobs. Suggest that the children look for these and more jobs when the class visits the grocery store.

At the store, ask the produce attendant to show the children where the fruits and vegetables are received and stored, the ways they are weighed and priced, and finally how they are arranged on the shelves for the customer. Continue the same procedure in the meat, dairy, and packaged-foods departments.

When the children return to the preschool or classroom, encourage each child to draw a picture of something new he or she discovered about how food is prepared for the customer at the grocery store. Arrange for adult volunteers or older children to help each child record a sentence or two about his or her picture.

Compile all of the drawings to make a class book to enjoy at storytime. As you read the page each child created, invite that child to stand and share another comment about the trip if he or she wishes to do so. Keep the book in the library center for the children to enjoy independently.

Visit a Bakery

"I know a baker is a special kind of chef."

Arrange for the class to visit a bakery. Be sure to obtain signed field-trip permission slips from the children's parents. Before the visit, help the children make a list of the different food items found in a bakery. Point out that besides making sweet foods like cakes and doughnuts, bakers also make loaves of bread, buns, rolls, and bagels. Point out that a baker is a special kind of chef who makes food items that belong in the bread and grain food group. Bread is an important part of our diet.

During the visit, ask the baker to show the children the large ovens and special bakery equipment. Caution the children about the need to keep their hands to themselves. If possible, invite the children to enjoy watching the baker decorate a special cake. When the children return to the classroom, invite them to dictate a thank-you letter to the baker. Encourage each child to "sign" the letter. It's okay if some children's handwriting is not legible.

Visit a Fast-Food Restaurant

"I know what the different workers do in a restaurant."

Arrange for the children to have a guided tour of a fast-food restaurant in your area. Be sure to obtain signed field-trip permission slips from the children's parents. Encourage the children to ask questions of their tour guide. Arrange to have a snack provided for the children by the fast-food restaurant, if possible.

Before the tour, remind the children not to touch equipment or food preparation areas in the restaurant because it is important to keep these areas very clean. Also remind the children of the importance of washing their hands and wearing aprons when handling food.

When the children return to the preschool or classroom, have them dictate a special thank-you letter to the employees of the fast-food restaurant. Encourage all of the children to "sign" the letter. It's okay if some of the children's names are not quite legible.

Whistle Stop Junction

The children will learn about trains and how trains, as one form of transportation, serve the community.

"I know the engine of a train has an important job."

"I know trains pick up and deliver other train cars to different places."

"I know a passenger train takes people to special places."

"I know I need a ticket to ride the train."

"I know suitcases help us carry our belongings on a train trip."

"I can make a train."

"I know a train has many different kinds of cars."

"I know flat cars carry heavy things."

"I know every job at a train station is important."

"I can travel in the air, on the water, and on the land."

"I know trains come to our community."

"I know train rides can be exciting!"

OPENING ACTIVITIES

Fingerplay

The Train

Here is the train (make a fist with one hand),
And here is the track (extend your left arm straight out).
Whoo-Whoo forward,
Choo-Choo back (move your fist along your extended arm).
Here are the wheels,
Going clackety-clack (rotate your hands around each other).
Poof! goes the smoke,
From the big smokestack (move your hands up quickly in a
    mushroom shape).

Little Black Engine

"I know the engine of a train has an important job."

Invite the children to share what they know about trains. Make a list of the types of train cars the children mention. Point out the special function of the engine. Help the children discover that an engineer drives the train.

Invite the children to pretend to be a train. Encourage the children to decide what cars they would like to be. Choose one child to be the "engine." Help the children form a long line behind that child. Have each child hold on to the waist of the child in front of him or her. Encourage the "engine" to take the children all around the classroom, chugging and chanting the following poem:

Little engine, chug, chug, chug.
Little engine, chug, chug, chug.
Little engine pull the train, train, train.
Smokestack on your back, back, back, back.
Coming down the track, track, track, track.
Little engine pull the train. Woo! Woo!

Train Cars

"I know trains pick up and deliver other train cars to different places."

Ask the children if they know how trains help people, why trains go from town to town, why trains are different lengths, and how cars are added or removed from a train.

Invite the children to pretend to be a train. Explain that this train will go from town to town picking up other train cars filled with products for delivery to different places. Ask the children to sit in different areas of the room. Explain that each area of the room represents a different town and the children are train cars waiting to be added to the train.

Invite one child to role-play the engine. Encourage the "engine" to chug around the room, stopping to hook up to the "train cars." When the train is full, invite the children to take a trip down the hall. When the train returns to the room, have the "engine" begin dropping off "train cars" to different places in the room. A whistle adds excitement to the train experience and may be used each time the train stops to help the "cars" stop without bumping into one another. Teach the children the following poem to chant as they play train as well:

Little train, chugging down the track.
First it goes up, then it comes back.
Adding on (or dropping off) cars as it goes,
Little train just grows and grows!

Passenger Train

"I know a passenger train takes people to special places."

Materials
tables and chairs
two long tables
tickets

Explain that passenger trains move people from one place to another. Point out that special equipment, such as beds, seats, dining-room tables and chairs, and bathroom facilities, are found on passenger trains. Encourage children who have taken train trips to share their experiences with the rest of the group.

Invite the children to take an imaginary trip on a passenger train. Set up rows of chairs for the passenger car, tables and chairs for the dining car, and long tables for the sleeping car. Assign one child to role-play the engineer, two children to take tickets, and three to four children to serve food. Help the children decide on a special place to visit. Discuss what they might see along the way and how long it will take to get to their destination.

Invite the children to enjoy the pretend trip, complete with a dining experience and time to rest in the "beds." Encourage the children to describe the scenery they "see" along the way. Make stops to change roles and to pick up passengers and drop off passengers so the train doesn't become too crowded. Encourage all the children to have an opportunity to experience the different cars and jobs.

Tickets, Please

"I know I need a ticket to ride the train."

Materials
    construction paper
    felt-tip pen

Make train tickets from various colors of construction paper. Print numerals, letters, or names on each ticket as well. Make a duplicate set. Help the children come up with a list of different places where tickets are needed—movies, fair rides, bus rides, circuses, plays, and so on. Point out that tickets often have special information on them. For example, some tickets have seat numbers, row numbers, and dates printed on them. If possible, show the children some examples of real tickets. Draw attention to the differences in details of each one.

Help the children arrange their chairs in rows to represent seats on a train. Put one set of construction-paper tickets on a "ticket" table. Tape the duplicate set of tickets to the backs of the children's chairs. Explain that to ride this train, the children must first pick up boarding tickets. As the children board the train, help them find their seats by matching their boarding tickets with the tickets taped to the chairs. Once the train is full, collect the tickets from the "passengers." Check both sets of tickets to make sure the children are sitting in the correct spaces.

CENTER ACTIVITIES

Suitcase

"I know suitcases help us carry our belongings on a train trip."

Materials
>   suitcase and items to pack
>   travel tags
>   shoeboxes (ask each child to bring one from home)
>   spray paint
>   newspaper
>   cord or rope
>   various colors and sizes of construction paper
>   scissors
>   felt-tip pens or crayons
>   electrical tape
>   map of the United States

Pack a suitcase from home with clothes and other travel items to take on a train trip. Bring the suitcase to school and set it in a prominent place in the room. Encourage the children to predict what is in the suitcase. Then unpack it. Set the items on a table. Ask the children if they can predict where you might take a trip based on the items packed. Did you pack warm clothes? Did you include beachwear?

Invite the children to help repack the suitcase. Point out that there is a special way to pack items so space is not wasted. Once the items are packed, invite different children to try and lift the suitcase. Point out how heavy the items are now that they are packed in the suitcase all together. Write the name of your destination on a travel tag and tie the tag onto the handle of the suitcase. Explain that the suitcase is put in a special compartment on the train. The tag tells the baggage workers to take the suitcase out of the baggage compartment at a particular train station.

Invite the children to make suitcases to pack for a trip they might like to take. Send a note home asking parents to send a shoebox with their child and include a brief explanation of the activity. Show the children a map of the United States. Help the children choose a place to go. Discuss the weather, the types of sight-seeing opportunities available, and other important information about the place chosen. Then help the children come up with a list of appropriate clothing and other items needed for the trip.

Write each child's name inside his or her shoebox and then invite the children to set their shoeboxes on a table covered with newspaper. Spray paint the outside of each shoebox. Caution children to stay away from the paint and paint fumes. While the children wait for the paint to dry, have them draw pictures or cut pictures from magazines of the various items they wish to pack in their suitcases. Remind the children to make tags for their suitcases as well.

When the shoeboxes are dry, use electrical tape to tape one side of the lids to the top section of the shoeboxes so that the shoeboxes open from one side like a real suitcase. To make a handle, have an adult volunteer poke two holes on either side of the shoebox, string a section of rope through the two holes, and tie each end of the rope in a knot to prevent the rope from slipping. Then invite the children to pack their suitcases with the items they have made. Have each child dictate to an adult volunteer the name of his or her destination so that each child may attach a tag to his or her suitcase handle. (This activity may take two consecutive days, depending on your schedule.)

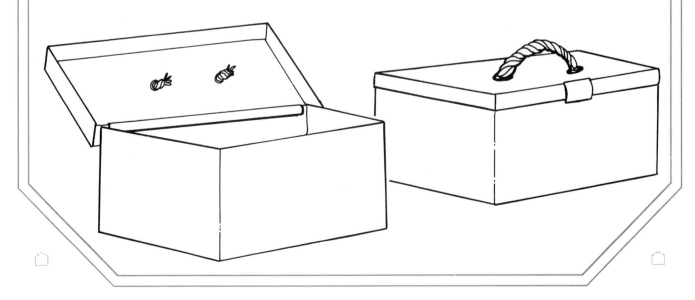

Simple Trains

"I can make a train."

Materials

    bottom sections of cardboard egg cartons (cut in half lengthwise)
    pipe cleaners
    tempera paints of various colors
    empty toilet-paper rolls (cut in half lengthwise)
    glue
    buttons
    masking tape
    scissors
    paintbrushes
    newspaper
    paint smocks

Invite the children to bring toy trains to school from home to share with the class. If available, invite an interested parent to share his or her train collection or electric train set with the children. Help the children name the different types of train cars. Point out the writing on the different cars as well. Explain that train models often show special details found on actual trains.

Invite the children to make models of trains using egg cartons. Have an adult volunteer cut the egg cartons in half lengthwise and poke small holes in each of the sections for the pipe cleaners. Give each child two half sections of an egg carton. Attach the two sections together with a pipe cleaner so each child has a train twice the length of the original carton. Show the children how to glue half toilet-paper rolls over one end of the egg carton trains to make engines.

Next, suggest that the children paint each of their "train cars" (egg cups) a different color. When the paint dries, encourage the children to paint numbers and letters on some of the cars with white paint. Finally, show the children how to glue buttons on for wheels. Make train tracks on the classroom floor with masking tape. Invite the children to take their trains for a ride down the tracks!

Train Mural

"I know a train has many different kinds of cars."

Materials
   train engine made from construction paper
   construction paper
   train-car patterns
   black construction paper cut in 4" x 4" squares
   felt-tip pens or crayons
   scissors
   stapler
   old magazines
   glue

Read *Freight Train* by Donald Crews (see the bibliography on page 93).
Show the children the special illustrations. Help the children make a list
of the cars that are mentioned in the book—hopper car, gondola car,
and so on. Then encourage the children to come up with a list of items
that could be carried in the train cars, such as cows or lumber. Write
each list on chart paper for the children to see, even though they may
not be able to read the words. Encourage the children to list how trains
are a special help to a community. Help the children discover that trains
are able to carry larger amounts of products at one time than airplanes
or trucks.

   Pin a construction-paper train engine on a bulletin board. Give each
child a sheet of construction paper and a train-car pattern. Help the
children trace the train-car patterns on the construction paper. Invite
the children to cut out the train-car shapes. Show the children how to
make wheels to glue on each of their cars by rounding the corners of the
black squares of construction paper. Staple each car behind the engine
on the bulletin board to make a long train. Invite the children to "load"
the train cars with products by drawing their own pictures or by cutting
out pictures of products from old magazines and gluing them on the
various cars.

Delicious Flat Cars

"I know flat cars carry heavy things."

Materials

    celery stalks cut into 4" lengths
    peanut butter
    round crackers
    raisins (optional)
    butter knives
    pretzel sticks

Explain that there are special cars on a train called *flat cars*. These cars carry farming equipment, construction equipment, and other heavy machinery. Help the children come up with a list of other items that flat cars might carry.

Show the children the round crackers, celery sections, peanut butter, and pretzel sticks. Invite the children to share ways these items could be used to make a model of a flat car. Point out that the crackers resemble wheels and the celery might represent a flat car. Be sure the children wash their hands before this activity since they will be handling food.

Give each child four round crackers (with little holes cut through each one), pretzels, and a celery stick. Show the children how to attach the crackers to the ends of the pretzel sticks to make the wheels and axles. Invite the children to spread peanut butter on the celery sticks (raisins are optional) and then set the celery on top of the axles. Suggest that each child make several flat cars to form a mini-train. Invite the children to enjoy a terrific train treat together!

Train Dramatic Play

"I know every job at a train station is important."

Help the children make a list of the jobs required to run a train station—ticket agents, conductor, engineer, baggage checkers, porters, and so on. Discuss each job as well. Show the children different dramatic-play items, such as those suggested on page 65 and help the children decide how each item would be used.

Arrange the children's chairs in rows to represent the seating on a train. Invite the children to decide where to place the items in order to set up a pretend train station. Select children to role-play the various jobs. Explain that the engineer wears a special hat, drives the train, and determines the destination. The conductor wears a special uniform, helps passengers find their seats, punches tickets, and announces the destinations.

The ticket agents sell boarding tickets. In addition, there are clerks to answer the phone, baggage checkers to tag the luggage, and porters to help carry bags. The passengers purchase boarding tickets, carry their baggage to the train, and then ride. Invite the children to sing travel songs, such as "Down by the Station," as they pretend to ride through the countryside.

Suggested Props for a Train Station Dramatic-Play Area

variety of hats for passengers and ticket agents
engineer hat and neckerchief
hat and vest for conductor
recipe cards for tickets
hole punch
telephone
chairs
suitcases

Transportation Chart

"I can travel in the air, on the water, and on the land."

Materials
- large posterboard
- construction paper (12" x 18" sheets)
- magazine pictures of different forms of transportation
- felt-tip pens or crayons
- glue
- scissors
- masking tape

This activity may be more appropriate for older children. Help the children make a list of as many different forms of transportation as possible. Explain that every form of transportation may be grouped as either transportation by land, water, or air. Divide a large piece of posterboard into three sections. Label the first section "Land," the middle section "Water," and the last section "Air."

Show the children a picture of a motor vehicle, boat, train, airplane, bicycle, or another type of transportation. Help the children decide if the picture shows travel on land, water, or in the air. Place the picture on the chart in the appropriate section. Place a piece of masking tape on the back of several pictures and give a picture to each child. Invite each child to place his or her picture on the chart in the correct section.

Encourage the children to make their own transportation charts. Help each child fold a piece of construction paper into three sections. Invite the children to draw the correct transportation pictures for each section. Then suggest that the children cut out pictures of different forms of transportation to glue on their charts.

OUTDOOR ACTIVITIES

Observe a Train

"I know trains come to our community."

Most communities have a train network connecting their community with other communities. Call the local train information center to get approximate times trains travel near your area. Plan to take the class on a walk to a train station or crossing where the children may view first-hand the different train cars and the special products the cars carry. Be sure to obtain signed field-trip permission slips from the children's parents.

Before the walk, discuss safety precautions children need to follow when crossing train tracks or while waiting for a train to pass by. Emphasize the importance of staying a good distance from a moving train to avoid injury from flying rocks or debris. Discuss the different safety equipment that is provided at each train crossing, such as the signal arm that holds back traffic, the blinking lights, and the warning signs posted near train crossings. Encourage the children to discuss the purpose of the different pieces of safety equipment.

Signal arms—are provided at train crossings on very busy roads. The signal arm is lowered to block the road so cars cannot cross the train tracks when a train passes by.

Blinking lights—are provided at train crossings on busy roads. The lights blink on and off to warn the cars that a train will be crossing soon.

Warning signs—are provided at train crossings on roads that are not busy. The warning signs tell cars to stop and look both ways to see if a train is coming before crossing the tracks.

When the train approaches, help the children count the cars. Encourage the children to listen to the sounds of the train and wave to the engineer or other train personnel.

All Aboard!

"I know train rides can be exciting!"

Invite those children in your classroom who have ridden on trains to share their experiences with the rest of the class. If a commuter train is available in your area, arrange for the children to experience a train ride firsthand. Be sure to obtain signed field-trip permission slips from the children's parents. If possible, ask a representative from the commuter train station to meet the children at the station and answer any questions the children may have before boarding the train. Ask the guide to give any needed directions concerning safety while boarding and exiting the train, too.

Community Celebrations

The children will celebrate events that bring the community closer together as they continue to work with one another.

"I know the flag is red, white, and blue."
"I can march in a circus parade."
"I can make a community picture."
"I can make muffins for a community bake sale."
"I can help keep the Earth healthy."
"I can help plant a tree."

OPENING ACTIVITIES

Fingerplay

A Bit O' Botany

It's fun to climb the trees outside (hand-over-hand climbing motion),
They stand so tall and strong (raise arms).
The lawn of grass hides anthills well (extend fingers),
Each blade so green and long.
Vines that look like leafy ropes
Up the tree trunks crawl (fingers crawl up arm).
Bushes look like little trees (one arm down, other arm straight up
    to form a tree)
Without a trunk at all (lower arm until fingers touch horizontal arm).

Song

"The Neighborhood"
(Sung to the tune of "Here We Go 'Round the Mulberry Bush")

Let's clean up the neighborhood,
The neighborhood,
The neighborhood.
Let's clean up the neighborhood,
And work all together.

Why don't we plant a tree,
Plant a tree,
Plant a tree?
Why don't we plant a tree,
to help the Earth stay healthy?

This is my community.
Community,
Community.
This is my community,
And we like to work together!

CENTER ACTIVITIES

Patriotic Parade

"I know the flag is red, white, and blue."

Materials
  red, white, and blue streamers
  American flag
  record player or cassette tape player
  marching music

Select a child to help hold the American flag for all the children to see. Focus the children's attention on the three flag colors. Explain that the first American flag was made with these three colors. Red, white, and blue are the patriotic colors of the United States. If you have children in your classroom from other countries, invite these children to share information about their countries' flags and colors as well.

Help the children name occasions when the American flag is shown (Flag Day, Veteran's Day, Fourth of July, parades) or special times when red, white, and blue colors are used for decoration (Fourth of July).

Invite the children to march in a patriotic parade. Give each child a colored streamer to carry. Help the children form a long line. Then play some marching music and lead the children in a march around the classroom, inviting them to carry their streamers high above their heads. After the parade, invite the children to recite or listen as you say the Pledge of Allegiance. Encourage the children to stand facing the flag with their right hands over their hearts.

Pledge of Allegiance

I pledge allegiance to the flag of the United States of America and to the Republic for which it stands, one Nation under God, indivisible, with liberty and justice for all.

Clown Parade

"I can march in a circus parade."

Materials
    circus music
    record player

Invite the children to describe the sights and sounds of a circus parade. Encourage the children to focus on the different types of animals and people that are usually found in a circus parade, especially the clowns and the special outfits clowns wear. Ask the children to describe how a circus makes them feel as well. Help the children discover how the community benefits from having a circus come to town.

Invite the children to pretend to put on clown clothes, such as oversized shoes, a red nose, face paint, pants with suspenders, and so on. Play marching music or special circus music for the children to march to as you lead them in a circus parade around the classroom. Encourage the children to imagine the townspeople watching the parade. Suggest that the children wave to imaginary spectators as they march.

Art Fair

"I can make a community picture."

Materials
  white sheets of paper
  construction paper
  cardboard
  tape
  scissors
  glue
  crayons or felt-tip markers

Give each child a sheet of white paper. Explain to the children that they are going to have a community art fair. Invite the children to create any kind of picture that they want. Encourage the children to draw a tree, a friend, or just make designs on their papers. If they want, the children may glue pieces of construction paper on their white sheets of paper.

Cut the cardboard into 8" x 2" strips—one for each child. Write "By (child's name)" on each strip with a dark-colored felt-tip marker. After the children have finished making their pieces of art, tape each picture on the wall or place the pictures flat on the table in the classroom art center. Place the cardboard strips with the children's names underneath the appropriate pictures. Take the children on a "tour" of their community art fair. Invite parents, guardians, or other classes to tour the art fair as well.

Bake Sale

"I can make muffins for a community bake sale."

Materials
- muffin tins
- pot holders
- aprons
- mixing spoons
- bowls
- measuring spoons
- measuring cups
- wax paper or cooling rack
- plastic bags

Invite children to guess how much a baby tree might cost. Explain to the children that they can earn the money they need to buy a tree seedling that they can plant.

Arrange for permission to have a bake sale at school. Send a letter home to parents letting them know of the date and purpose of the sale. Ask parents if they would like to contribute cookies, cakes, and so on and if they would like to come to the bake sale as well.

Invite the children to help you design a flyer for the bake sale. Use 8 1/2" x 11" paper so it can be easily copied and distributed. Ask the children to help decorate posters for the event to post around the preschool, school, and neighborhood. Make muffins for the bake sale with the children. Remind the children to wash their hands and wear aprons before they cook. Be sure to keep the children away from the hot oven.

Note: This activity goes along with the *Arbor Day* activity on pages 78 and 79.

Apple Raisin-Bran Muffins

4 cups Raisin Bran cereal	Preheat the oven to 400°. Grease the muffin cups.
2 cups chopped apples	Have an adult volunteer help the children measure
2 1/2 cups all-purpose flour	and combine the cereal, apples, flour, sugar, baking
1 cup sugar	soda, and salt in a large bowl. Stir in the
2 1/2 tsp baking soda	buttermilk, eggs, and oil and mix thoroughly. Do not
1 1/2 tsp salt	over mix. Spoon batter into greased tins, about 2/3
2 cups buttermilk	full. Bake for approximately 20 minutes, or until
2 eggs, beaten	lightly browned. Remove the muffins onto a cooling
1/2 cup vegetable oil	rack or onto wax paper. Caution the children to not
	touch the muffins until they are properly cooled.
	This recipe should make 12 muffins. Be sure the
	children wash their hands. Once the muffins have
	cooled, have the children count out four muffins.
	Have the children place each set of four muffins in
	a plastic bag to sell at the bake sale.

OUTDOOR ACTIVITIES

Earth Day

"I can help keep the Earth healthy."

Materials
- paper grocery bags
- disposable plastic gloves
- empty pop or soda can
- empty pop or soda bottle
- egg carton
- plastic detergent bottle
- small pile of newspaper

Explain to the children that Earth Day is celebrated every year on April 22nd, but we should make every day Earth Day to help keep the Earth healthy. Invite the children to name ways in which we can help the Earth. Write responses on the chalkboard. Ask the children if they know what the word *recycle* means. Explain that recycle means to reuse or to use again. Show the children each of the items collected for this activity. Point out that each of these items can be used again. Describe ways that the children can help recycle items at home and at school.

Give each child a paper grocery bag. Take the children outside on the school grounds or to a nearby park. If you go to a nearby park, be sure to obtain signed field-trip permission slips from the children's parents. Send a note home to the parents explaining the purpose of this activity. Tell the children that one very simple way to help keep the Earth healthy is to help keep it clean. Give each child a set of disposable plastic gloves to wear while picking up trash. Encourage the children to pick up any trash that they see and put the trash in their paper grocery bags. (Be sure you have adult volunteers along to monitor this activity.) Bring along an extra grocery bag for yourself. Urge the children to put anything they think is recyclable, such as plastic soda pop bottles, cans, and so on, in your grocery bag.

Arbor Day

"I can help plant a tree."

Materials
- tree seedling
- soil
- watering can
- water
- child-sized shovels or digging utensils

Use the money raised by the *Bake Sale* activity on page 75 to buy a tree seedling. Or, ask a tree nursery or an organization to donate a small tree seedling for planting by your students. Arrange for permission for your class to plant a tree on the school grounds or at a nearby lot or park.

Take the children outside and encourage them to look closely at the trees around them. Explain that birds make their nests in trees, squirrels eat nuts from trees, insects live on trees, and so on. Take the children to the designated area where you are going to plant the seedling. Tell the children that by planting a new tree, they are helping the Earth, birds, squirrels, and other living things.

Give each child a shovel or other digging utensil. Explain that soil needs to be loosened before the seedling can be planted. Invite the children to dig up the ground in a small area. Dig a hole large enough for all the roots to fit. Set the tree in the hole and cover the roots with soil. Encourage the children to help you pack the dirt firmly around the tree. Then allow each child to take a turn at watering the newly planted seedling. It may be helpful to set up a tree-watering schedule so that every other day or so a child is assigned to water the growing tree. This may be helpful to avoid over-watering as well. If possible, have the children check on the tree throughout it's first year.

Community Services

Children have the opportunity to meet important people in the community as well as learn about how a community works.

"I know there are a lot of community helpers in my school."

"I know how to dial 911."

"I know doctors and nurses help me get well in the hospital."

"I know what happens to my letters when I mail them."

"I know the library has lots of books for me to read."

"I can make a present for a special friend."

"I know that firefighters help me and my community."

"I know that police officers help me and my community."

"I know my community has parks I can play in."

OPENING ACTIVITIES

Fingerplay

Mail

Five little letters lying on a tray (extend fingers of right hand).
Mommy came in and took the first away (bend down thumb).
Then Daddy said, "This big one is for me."
I counted them twice, now there were three (bend down the
    pointer finger).
Brother Bill asked, "Did I get any mail?"
He found one and cried, "A letter from Gale (bend down middle finger)!"
My sister Jane took the next to the last,
And ran upstairs to open it fast (bend down ring finger).
As I can't read, I'm not able to see
Whom the last one's for, but I hope it's for me (wiggle the little finger,
    then clap hands)!

Song

"Going on a Picnic"
(Sung to the tune of "Down by the Station")

Going on a picnic,
Leaving right away.
If it doesn't rain, we'll stay all day.
Did you bring the sandwiches?
Yes, I brought the sandwiches.
Ready for a picnic, here we go.

Other Verses

Did you bring the melon?
Yes, I brought the melon.

Did you bring the apples?
Yes, I brought the apples.

CENTER ACTIVITIES

Helpers in Our School

"I know there are a lot of community helpers in my school."

Invite the children to name as many school helpers in their preschool or school as they can. Explain to the children that a school is very important to the community because schools teach children many things they need to know. Encourage the children to list things they have already learned in preschool or school. Invite a few people within the school to come and speak to the children about what they do within the school system.

Encourage the speakers to bring props or examples of their work with them to show the children. The art teacher could bring samples of art work, for example. The following is a list of possible people within the school system or preschool who could come and speak to the children. Use your own ideas as well. Of course, with this many visitors suggested, this activity may require several weeks. Children could possibly become overwhelmed with more than one visitor a day.

Kindergarten	Preschool
principal	director
physical education teacher	cook
art teacher	teacher
school secretary	van driver
music teacher	helper
custodian	custodian
school nurse	

Emergency

"I know how to dial 911."

old push-button phone
old dial phone

Ask the children if they know what an emergency is. Explain that an emergency is when we need help very quickly. Name emergencies, such as fire, an accident, or an illness. Explain to the children that if there is an emergency and there is no one available to help them, they should call "911" on the telephone. Tell children that whoever answers the phone when they call "911" will be able to help them. Explain that when they call "911" in an emergency, they are calling the police and the fire department in their community. Be sure to explain to the children that they must give their names and where they are calling from when they call "911" so the police or fire department can send someone to help them.

Show the children the telephones. Ask the children if they can find the numbers "911." Give each child a chance to push the "911" buttons on the phone. Ask the children if any of them have a dial phone at home. Show the children how to dial "911" as well. Also invite the children to practice saying their names, addresses, and phone numbers. Have that information available for each child so that you can provide information as needed.

Classroom Hospital

"I know doctors and nurses help me get well in the hospital."

Materials
- white sheet
- white shirts
- Red Cross headbands
- reusable bandages, splints, medical tape, slings, and other safe medical supplies
- child-size crutches
- cot
- small table
- dolls or stuffed animals

Invite the children to dress up and pretend they are doctors and nurses in a hospital. Remind the children that a boy or a girl can be a doctor and that a boy or a girl can be a nurse. Suggest that the children fix broken bones, bandage arms and legs, and pretend to take temperatures. Encourage the children to use dolls and stuffed animals for patients. If crutches are available, invite each of the children to try using them as well.

OUTDOOR ACTIVITIES

Let's Send a Letter

"I know what happens to my letters when I mail them."

Materials
    letter-sized paper
    crayons and felt-tip makers
    office-size envelopes
    stamps

Explain to the children that when we mail a letter, it first has to go to the post office before it goes to the person we are sending it to. Invite the children to make pictures to send to their families. As the children are creating their pictures, write each child's address on a long envelope. Or ask each child to dictate his or her address to you, if he or she knows it. Tell the children that every letter that is sent must have a stamp on it or the post office will not deliver the letter. Hand out one stamp to each child and help the children lick the stamps and stick them in the upper right-hand corners of the envelopes.

Arrange for the children to visit the local post office. Prior to the visit, be sure to obtain signed field-trip permission slips from the children's parents. Ask if the children can be given a tour. Bring the children's letters with you and have the postal employee show the children what happens to a letter after it has been mailed.

The next day, ask the class to dictate a thank-you letter to the postal workers at the local post office. Encourage each child to "sign" the letter. Then, as a group, take the letter to the nearest mailbox and mail it together.

Reading Time

"I know the library has lots of books for me to read."

Arrange for the class to attend a story hour at the local community library. Be sure to obtain signed field-trip permission slips from the children's parents. Ask if the library will give the children a short tour of the different library areas. Explain that you must have a library card to check out books from the library. Ask the children to raise their hands if they have a library card. If the library in your area does not have a story hour, ask permission to give your own story hour to the children at the library, if possible.

Senior Citizen Center Visit

"I can make a present for a special friend."

Arrange for the children to visit the local senior citizen center. Be sure to obtain signed field-trip permission slips from the children's parents. Before the visit, encourage the children to make placemats for the senior citizens. Directions are provided here. If possible, invite the children to share their favorite songs or fingerplays in a short program at the center.

Handprint Placemats

foil pie tins
various colors of tempera paint
construction paper
small sponges
paint smocks
containers of soapy water
paper towels
newspaper
felt-tip markers
crayons

Cover a table and work area with newspaper. Be sure the children wear paint smocks. Place foil pie tins with tempera paint and a sponge for each color on the newspaper-covered work table. Next, set out sheets of construction paper. Finally, place bowls of soapy water and paper towels at the end of the table. Invite the children to make handprint placemats. Have an adult volunteer help the children paint both hands using a sponge as a brush. Help the children place their paint-covered hands firmly on the construction paper in order to make clear prints. Have an adult volunteer help the children wash their hands in the soapy water and then label each child's handprint. Don't be surprised if a child does not want his or her hand painted. That's okay. Never force a child to do an activity that feels uncomfortable to him or her. When the placemats are dry, encourage the children to decorate their placemats with crayons or markers. Explain to the children that the placemats are going to be presents for some special friends.

Let's Visit the Fire Station

"I know that firefighters help me and my community."

Arrange to take the children on a field trip to a fire station. Be sure to obtain signed field-trip permission slips from the children's parents. Ask the firefighters to take the children on a tour of the station. Have your guide point out special firefighting equipment and explain the safety procedures used with each one. Encourage the guide to talk to the children about fire safety, including preventing fires. When the children return to the classroom, invite them to dictate a thank-you letter to the firefighters. Encourage each child to "sign" the letter before it is mailed.

Let's Visit the Police Station

"I know that police officers help me and my community."

Arrange for the children to visit the police station. Be sure to obtain signed field-trip permission slips from the children's parents. Prior to the visit, encourage the children to share what they know about police officers. Discuss the safety measures police officers use daily to keep the community safe. During the visit, ask the police officers to explain safety signs and the rules for safely crossing a street. When the children return to the classroom, invite them to dictate a thank-you note to the police officers. Encourage each child to "sign" the letter before mailing it.

A Picnic in the Park

"I know my community has parks I can play in."

Materials
    large blanket big enough for all the children to sit on
      (or two smaller ones)
    paper garbage bags
    sugar-free lemonade in a thermos or cooler
    paper cups

Send a letter home with the children asking the parents to prepare a sack lunch for their child on the date you specify for your picnic. Let the parents know that you will supply the drinks. Ask for parent volunteers to join you and your class on the picnic. Be sure to obtain signed field-trip permission slips from the children's parents.

Ask the children if they ever go to the park. Encourage them to make a list of all the things they can do at the park. Take the children to a park near the school. Ask them to help you pick out a perfect spot in the park for your picnic.

When a spot has been decided upon, invite the children to help you set up the picnic area. First, clear away any sticks or rocks. Then ask the children to gather any trash around the area. Encourage the children to save any trash they find if it is recyclable and put it in a separate trash bag.

When the spot is clear, have the children help you lay out blankets for everyone to sit on. Then sit together on the blankets and enjoy the picnic. After the picnic, invite the children to help you clean up any trash that is left over. Put the trash in paper bags and deposit the bags in a trash can.

Outcomes

Now that you and the children have explored, discovered, and connected with the theme of this resource, what types of outcomes can you expect?

Expect children to think:

"I know the dentist, police officer, and the firefighter are all important community helpers."

"I know how to cook some healthy foods that are good for me."

"I know trains are important to the community."

"I can take part in community celebrations."

Selected Children's Books

Children enjoy hearing good books read over and over again. The following books give the children opportunities to further explore the theme of this resource and establish an early love of reading. The books are listed by topic for your convenience. Share these stories with the children individually or in small groups.

Let's Play Dentist

Doctor De Soto, William Steig, Farrar, Straus and Giroux, 1982.

My Dentist, Harlow Rockwell, Greenwillow Books, 1975.

Richard Scarry's Busy, Busy World, Richard Scarry, Golden Press, 1965.

Teeth, John Gaskin, Franklin Watts, 1984.

When I Grow Up, Lois Lenski, Walck, 1960.

Little Chef

Apple Pigs, Ruth Orbach, Putnam Publishing Group, 1981.

Blue Bug's Vegetable Garden, Virginia Poulet, Childrens Press, 1973.

Blueberries for Sal, Robert McCloskey, Penguin, 1948.

The Complete Adventures of Peter Rabbit, Beatrix Potter, Warne, 1987.

Cranberry Thanksgiving, Wende and Harry Devlin, Macmillan, 1980.

The Popcorn Book, Tomie de Paola, Holiday, 1978.

Rain Makes Applesauce, Julian Scheer, Holiday, 1964.

Stone Soup, Marcia Brown, Macmillan, 1947.

The Very Hungry Caterpillar, Eric Carle, Putnam Publishing Group, 1981.

Whistle Stop Junction

Freight Train, Donald Crews, Greenwillow Books, 1978.

I Like Trains, Catherine Wodley, Hale, 1965.

The Little Engine That Could, Watty Piper, Buccaneer Books, 1981.

Trains, Byron Barton, Crowell, 1986.

Two Little Trains, Margaret Wise Brown, Addison-Wesley, 1949.

Community Celebrations

Fifty Simple Things Kids Can Do to Save the Earth, EarthWorks Group, Andrews and McMeel, 1990.

Community Services

Little Fireman, Margaret Wise Brown, Harper & Row, 1952.

Policeman Small, Lois Lenski, Walck, 1962.

Curious George Goes to the Hospital, H. A. and Margret Rey, Houghton Mifflin, 1966.

For Your Professional Library

The following books offer appropriate learning strategies and activities for the early-childhood learner. These materials may be used as additional resources for *Connecting with My Community.*

Resource Books

Creative Art for the Developing Child: A Teacher's Handbook for Early Childhood Education, 2nd edition, Clare Cherry, Fearon Teacher Aids, Simon & Schuster Supplementary Education Group, 1972.

Curriculum Planning for Young Children, edited by Janet F. Brown, National Association for the Education of Young Children, 1982.

Finger Frolics, compiled by Liz Cromwell and Dixie Hibner, Partner Press, 1976.

The Illustrated Treasury of Children's Literature, edited by Margaret E. Martignoni, compiled by P. Edward Ernest, Grosset and Dunlap, 1955.

Is the Left Brain Always Right? A Guide to Whole Child Development, Clare Cherry, Fearon Teacher Aids, Simon & Schuster Supplementary Education Group, 1989.

Resources for Creative Teaching in Early Childhood Education, Bonnie Mack Flemming and Darlene Softley Hamilton, Harcourt Brace Jovanovich, 1977.

Think of Something Quiet: A Guide for Achieving Serenity in Early Childhood Classrooms, Clare Cherry, Fearon Teacher Aids, Simon & Schuster Supplementary Education Group, 1981.

Where the Sidewalk Ends, Shel Silverstein, Harper & Row, 1974.

Children's Songbooks

Circle Time Activities for Young Children, Deya Brashears and Sharon Werlin, Starlite Printing, 1981.

Do Your Ears Hang Low? Fifty More Fingerplays, Tom Glazer, Doubleday and Company, 1980.

Eye Winker, Tom Tinker, Chin Chopper: Fifty Musical Fingerplays, Tom Glazer, Doubleday and Company, 1972.

The Great Song Book: A Collection of the Best-Loved Songs in the English Language, illustrated by Tomi Ungerer, Doubleday and Company, 1975.

Mockingbird Flight, Patricia Haglund Nielsen, Floyd Sucher, and Charlotte G. Garman, Economy Company, 1975.

The Raffi-Christmas Treasury: Fourteen Illustrated Songs and Musical Arrangements, Nadine Bernard Westcott, Crown Publishers, 1983.

The Raffi Singable Songbook, Raffi, Crown, 1980.

Songs I Can Play: For the Early Beginner, Ada Richter, Warner Brothers Publications, 1975.

Treasury of Songs for Children, Tom Glazer, Songs Music, 1964.